SOUTHERN FRIED

by
John Heine
and
Ellen Patrick

CRANE HILL
PUBLISHERS

Copyright © 1998 by John Heine and Ellen Patrick

All rights reserved. With the exception of brief quotations in critical reviews or articles, no part of this work may be reproduced or transmitted in any form or by any means, electronic or mechanical, including photo-copying, recording, or any information storage and retrieval system, without permission in writing from the publisher.

Printed in the United States of America
Published by Crane Hill Publishers, 3608 Clairmont Avenue, Birmingham, AL 35222; www.cranehill.com

Library of Congress Cataloging-in-Publication Data

Heine, John, 1950-
Southern fried / John Heine, Ellen Patrick.
p.   cm.
ISBN 1-57587-095-9 (TP)
1. Southern States—Social life and customs—Caricatures and cartoons. 2. American wit and humor. Pictorial.
I. Patrick, Ellen, 1951-   . II. Title.
NC1429.H377A4 1998
741.5'973—dc21
                                                                                        98-40831
                                                                                                        CIP

10   9   8   7   6   5   4   3   2   1

the South is a State of Mind

YOU GOT THAT Right.

2

SOUTHERN FRIED

LOOKS LIKE DEE & THERMOND ARE BACK FROM THE RACES.

4

SOUTHERN
FRIED

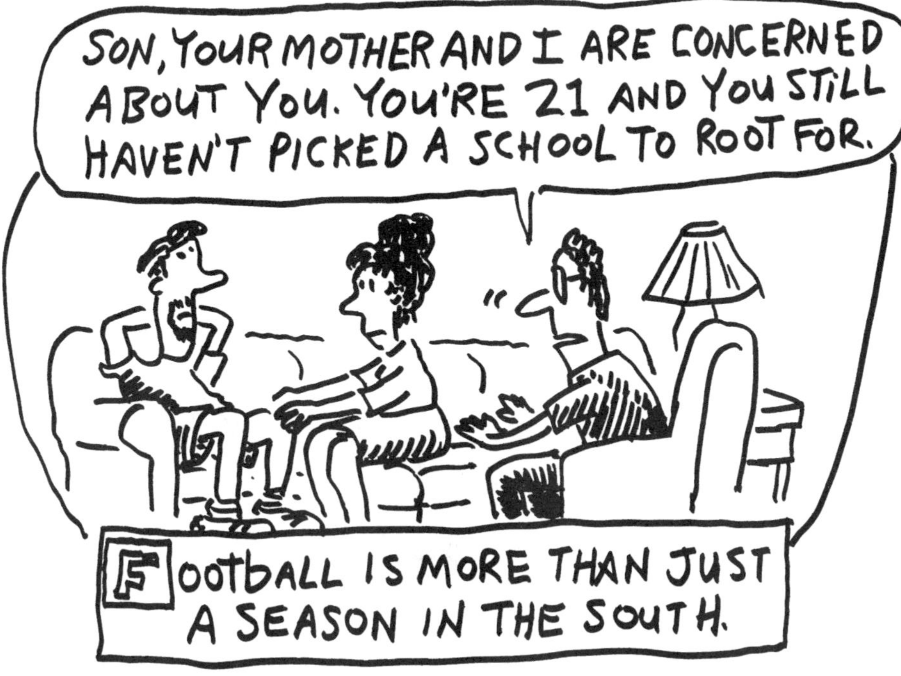

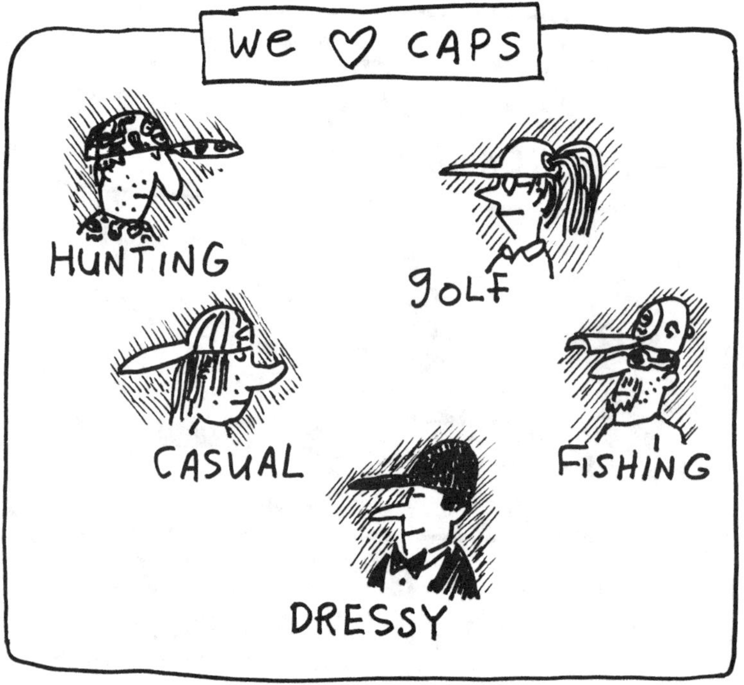
WE ♡ CAPS
HUNTING
GOLF
CASUAL
FISHING
DRESSY

SOUTHERN FRIED

Forgotten Inventions of the South

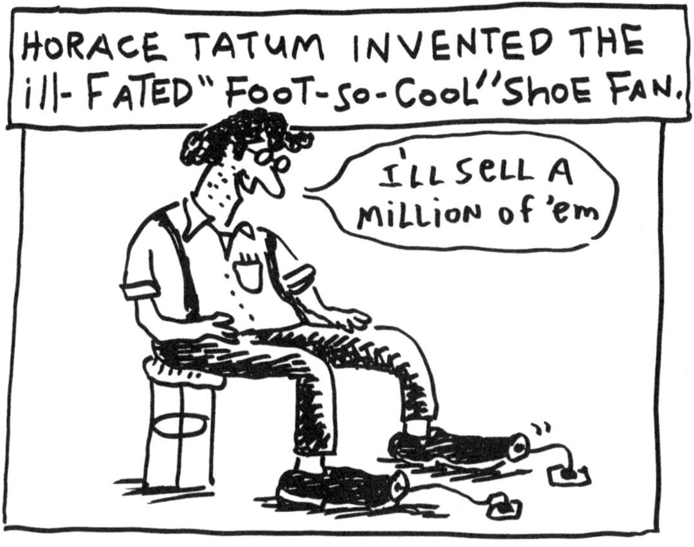

A guy + his Porch
HeLLo. This is MY PORCH. ISN'T IT GREAT!
I LIKE TO JUST SIT ON IT & LET THE WORLD GO BY.
NEXT TO GETTING FRISKY WITH MY WIFE, THIS PORCH IS MY FAVORITE THING.

SOUTHERN FRIED

a *guy* + his Porch

I REALLY LOVE PORCHES!

Here's the Design for my NEW PORCH.

..But I'm not sure if it's BIG enough.

House

Porch

All you Can Eat

19

Local Color

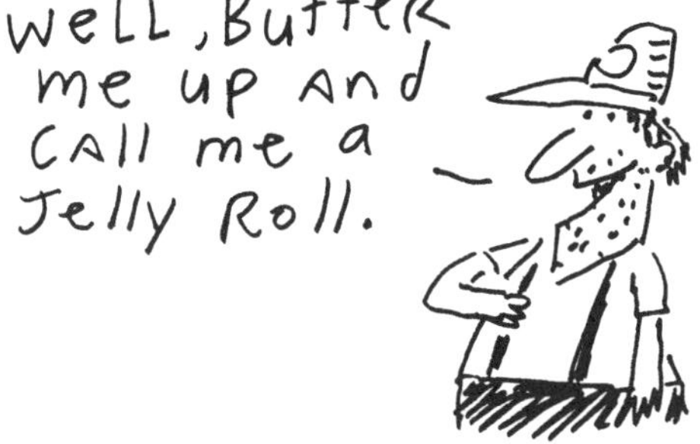

27

31

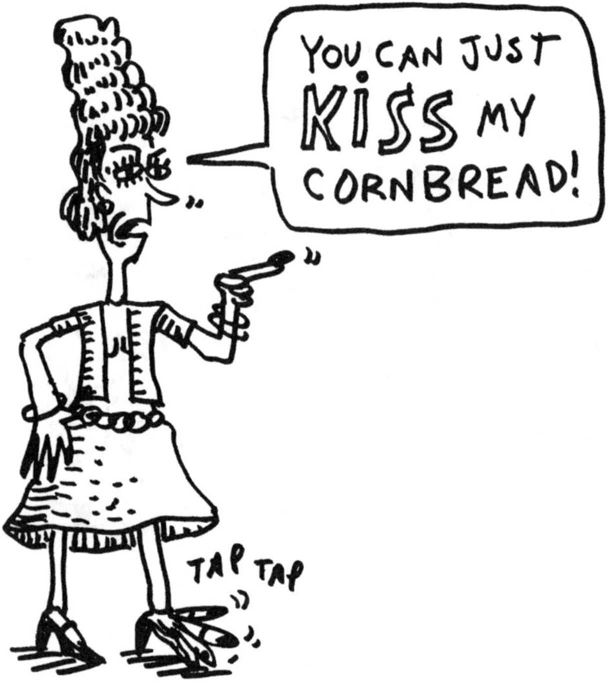
YOU CAN JUST KISS MY CORNBREAD!
TAP TAP

where the heck R we?

35

39

Rain or Shine

45

IN THE SOUTH, THE SUMMERS
REALLY STICK TO YOU.

48

Ammo & Camo

53

MYTHS OF THE SOUTH
IN SPITE OF WHAT MOST PEOPLE THINK, MOST SOUTHERN GUYS KNOW ALMOST NOTHING ABOUT FIXING CARS.
I DON'T KNOW. WHAT DO YOU THINK IS WRONG?

MYTHs of the South

ALL MANSIONS WITH COLUMNS ARE NOT NECESSARILY HAUNTED.

Myths of the South

CONTRARY TO POPULAR THINKING SOUTHERNERS DON'T BLEED BAR-B-Q SAUCE.

MYths of the south

THE TRUTH IS ONLY A SMALL PERCENTAGE OF PEOPLE IN THE SOUTH EVER WEAR ANY TYPE OF CAMOUFLAGE CLOTHING.

It's not mine. I found it on the side of the road.

See Rock City

WHICH ONE IS THE
PECKERWOOD?

PICK ONE

A.

B.

SOUTHERN FRIED

This ought to be interesting

FIRE ANTS

RAYMOND TAKES THE "FIGHT FIRE ANTS WITH FIRE ANTS" APPROACH TO LAWN CARE.

76

SOUTHERN FRIED

OPRAH MAKES TV HISTORY WHEN SHE DOES HER SHOW FROM THE BOTTOM OF A KENTUCKY MINE SHAFT.

HELLO KENTUCKY

SOUTHERN
FRIED

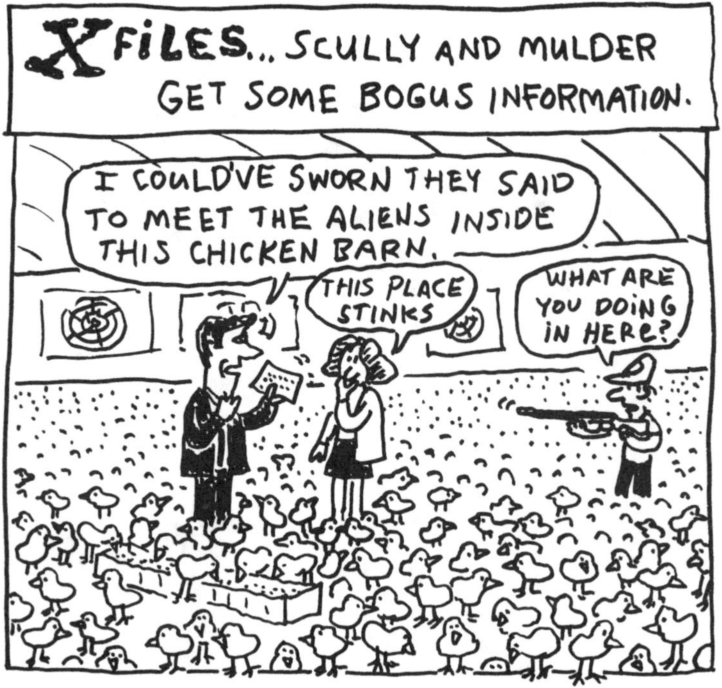

UNUSUAL school MASCOTS

FRIED GREEN TOMATOES! FRIED GREEN TOMATOES! IT'S ALWAYS FRIED GREEN TOMATOES! CAN'T WE JUST ONCE HAVE PLAIN TOMATOES?!